U.S. $5.95
CAN. $8.95

Mary Ann Shadd Cary spent her entire life fighting for justice and equality for black Americans. Born free and black in 1823, Mary Ann grew up believing that she was as good as anyone—black or white. Mary Ann started schools, wrote books and articles, and became the first black woman to publish a weekly newspaper and to enter law school. Mary Ann Shadd Cary was never afraid of offending anyone. She simply demanded justice for herself and her fellow black Americans.

Other Carolrhoda Creative Minds titles:

Civil Rights Pioneer
A Story about Mary Church Terrell

Dance of the Swan
A Story about Anna Pavlova

Freedom Seeker
A Story about William Penn

Germ Hunter
A Story about Louis Pasteur

Liberty or Death
A Story about Patrick Henry

President of the Underground Railroad
A Story about Levi Coffin

Remember the Ladies
A Story about Abigail Adams

Seneca Chief, Army General
A Story about Ely Parker

Sisters against Slavery
A Story about Sarah and Angelina Grimké

Voice of Freedom
A Story about Frederick Douglass

With Open Hands
A Story about Biddy Mason

Writing for Freedom
A Story about Lydia Maria Child

For more information about these and othees, call 800-328-4929 or visit w

ISBN 0-87614-928-X

9 780876 149287   50595

First Avenue Ed
An imprint of
Lerner Publishing

A Creative Minds Biography

DEMANDING JUSTICE

A Story about Mary Ann Shadd Cary

by Jeri Chase Ferris

illustrations by Kimanne Smith

Jeri Chase Ferris
4-10

Carolrhoda Books, Inc./Minneapolis

For my dear daughter-in-law Cindi, a fighter for justice; my dear son, Tom; and their beautiful children Cara and Jack
—*J.C.F.*

With thanks to the family of Mary Ann Shadd Cary; Dr. Berky Nelson, UCLA, and Dr. Jane Rhodes, UCSD, for their guidance; the staffs at Howard University, Smith College, Tulane University, the Ontario Black History Society, and the Chatham-Kent Public Library; American and Canadian libraries and museum staff; and my editor, Susan Rose

Text copyright © 2003 by Jeri Chase Ferris
Illustrations copyright © 2003 by Kimanne Smith

This book is available in two editions:
Library binding by Carolrhoda Books, Inc., a division of Lerner Publishing Group
Soft cover by First Avenue Editions, an imprint of Lerner Publishing Group
241 First Avenue North
Minneapolis, MN 55401 U.S.A.

Website address: www.lernerbooks.com

Library of Congress Cataloging-in-Publication Data

Ferris, Jeri.
    Demanding justice : a story about Mary Ann Shadd Cary / by Jeri Chase Ferris ; illustrated by Kimanne Smith.
        p.   cm. — (A creative minds biography)
    Summary: Describes the life of Mary Ann Shadd Cary, nineteenth-century educator, writer, newspaper editor, and civil rights worker who was the first African-American woman to enter law school or to publish a newspaper.
    Includes bibliographical references and index.
        ISBN: 1–57505–177–X (lib. bdg. : alk. paper)
        ISBN: 0–87614–928–X (pbk. : alk. paper)
    1. Cary, Mary Ann Shadd, 1823–1893—Juvenile literature. 2. African American women civil rights workers—Biography—Juvenile literature. 3. Civil rights workers—United States—Biography—Juvenile literature. 4. African Americans—Civil rights—History—19th century—Juvenile literature. 5. Free African Americans—Biography—Juvenile literature. 6. Newspaper editors—United States—Biography—Juvenile literature. 7. Educators—Canada—Biography—Juvenile literature. [1. Cary, Mary Ann Shadd, 1823–1893. 2. Educators. 3. Civil rights workers. 4. African Americans—Biography. 5. Women—Biography.] I. Smith, Kimanne, ill. II. Title. III. Series.
E185.97.C32 F47 2003
305.48'896073'0092—dc21   2002006815

Manufactured in the United States of America
1 2 3 4 5 6 – MA – 08 07 06 05 04 03

Table of Contents

Introduction   5

Growing Up   6

Saying What She Thinks   14

Canada   19

A Terrible Year   28

A Newspaper of Her Own   35

Change and More Change   46

A New Life   53

Afterword   59

Map of Mary Ann's World   60

Selected Bibliography   61

Index   63

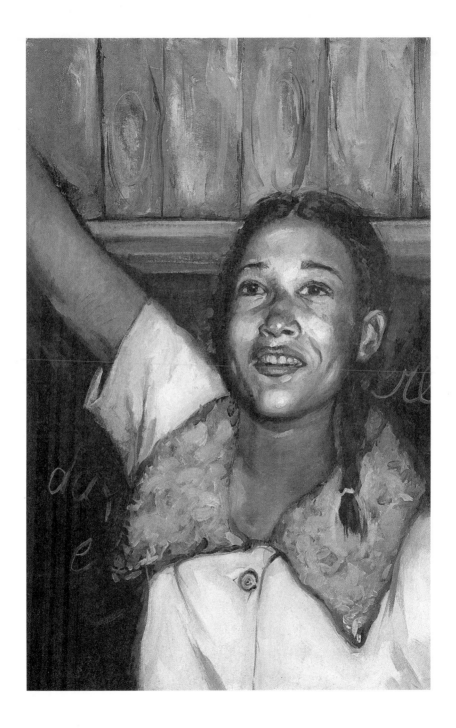

Introduction

Mary Ann Shadd Cary was born in 1823. She was black, and she was living at a time when many black Americans were held as slaves. But Mary Ann and her family had always been free. They worked hard for themselves, not for a slave master.

However, even though they were free, they did not have the rights and freedoms of white Americans. Mary Ann decided to fight for those rights for herself and her people.

She was the first black woman to publish a weekly newspaper. She was the first black woman to enter law school. She started schools. She wrote articles and books. She believed in self-reliance. She said what she thought, and she would not back down. She argued with just about everybody. She demanded justice for black Americans.

1

Growing Up

Mary Ann's great-grandfather, Hans Schad, a white man, had come from Germany to America in 1755. Here, he married Elizabeth Jackson, a black woman—a *free* black woman. Elizabeth and her family were free, as were hundreds of other hardworking black families, perhaps because they had escaped from slavery. Or perhaps they had been freed. Or perhaps they had not been brought from Africa as slaves at all, but had come by themselves from the West Indies.

The Shadd family settled in Delaware in the 1770s. In the 1820s, when Mary Ann was little, her father, Abraham Shadd, ran his shoemaking business in Wilmington, a busy town on the Brandywine River. Mary Ann's mother, Harriet Shadd, raised the children.

Because Abraham Shadd was black, he could not leave Delaware for more than six months, or he could never return. Free blacks from other states were forbidden to enter Delaware to visit the Shadds or anyone else. Mr. Shadd could be jailed if he was within half a mile of an election booth on election day. And of course every free black person had to carry the papers to prove they were free.

The Shadds didn't have an ordinary life, and they weren't an ordinary family. Mr. Shadd was an abolitionist, a person who wanted to abolish, or end, slavery. He was one of twelve black people in Wilmington who helped escaping slaves. His shop was a station on the Underground Railroad—which was not a railroad at all. It was a chain of safe places from the slave states north all the way to Canada. In a safe house like the Shadds', fleeing slaves could hide in the cellar or in a secret room while slave catchers searched in vain.

No doubt many of the runaway slaves were given shoes for their journey made by Mr. Shadd and food cooked by Mrs. Shadd. No doubt little Mary Ann helped carry blankets and clothes to the runaways.

She saw exhausted men and women and terrified children just her age. She knew they were running for their lives. Her heart pounded in fear for them, and for her mother and father. They would be put in prison or worse if runaway slaves were found in their house. Why was it, she wondered, that white people were free and so many black people were not?

Mary Ann was only four when her father began talking about a new and disagreeable idea he'd heard in town. It seems that some whites who said they were against slavery were also saying that free black people in Delaware should move to Africa. The whites didn't want blacks to associate with them. They did not think of blacks as equals.

But I *am* equal, Mary Ann surely thought. She already knew she was as smart as anyone else. Maybe smarter. Of course she was as good as anyone else. Maybe better.

No, her father surely said. Not better. Equal.

And as for going to Africa? Never, said Mr. Shadd. "We have rights in common with other Americans."

Mr. Shadd was a leader in the many conventions held by black men "for the bettering of our condition." Mary Ann heard what these men said, too. Some said black people could live without fear in Canada where everyone was free. But others said it wasn't right for free blacks to leave anyone behind in slavery. And a few, like Mr. Shadd, said black people could prove that they were as good as anyone else, so white people would see that slavery was wrong.

Mary Ann probably thought about these ideas while she buttoned her shoes, helped her mother bake bread and shell peas, washed her little brother's face, and changed her baby sister's diaper. She probably thought about them as she walked past the free public school (for whites only).

Mr. Shadd paid taxes for the public schools, but his children could not attend. Mary Ann's mother and father wanted their children to have a good education. They also decided it was safer to live where the laws for blacks weren't so unjust, so in 1833 they moved to West Chester, Pennsylvania, fifteen miles west of Philadelphia. Mr. Shadd found new customers and continued his work as a shoemaker, and Mrs. Shadd continued to raise their children.

Mary Ann was ten years old. By this time, she had three little sisters and one little brother. Would her family be safe in Pennsylvania?

Pennsylvania was a free state, but Philadelphia was not a friendly home for black people. In 1834 white mobs beat black people and burned their homes. In 1838 angry whites attacked the new Pennsylvania

Hall, built by abolitionists, and burned it to the ground.

In West Chester, though, Mary Ann was busy learning from her white teacher, Phoebe Darlington, who belonged to a religious and abolitionist group called the Quakers. Miss Darlington taught Mary Ann religion and literature, writing and math, Latin and French. At home, Mary Ann probably kept a book in one hand, a pen in the other, and practiced her French verbs out loud while she watched her little brothers and sisters.

In the small town of West Chester there were about three hundred hardworking free black people. In Philadelphia, just a buggy-ride away, there was a lively, active community of more than ten thousand free blacks.

Mary Ann could ride into Philadelphia with her father, who worked with abolitionist leaders there. She could take classes in music and dance, needlework and painting. She could have cake and lemonade with Philadelphia's well-to-do black teenagers at lectures and musical events. Mary Ann Shadd surely fit right in with the upper-class black society of Philadelphia, for she was self-confident, tall and slender, with soft light-brown skin, a lovely face, and sparkling eyes.

Mary Ann loved the excitement and culture of Philadelphia. It fit her energy and her impatient spirit, and she felt at home.

By the time she was sixteen, Mary Ann had learned all her Quaker teacher could teach. She did not want to be a cook, or a maid, or a washerwoman. She did not want to rent rooms to people for a living. She didn't want to be a homemaker like her mother. She now had eight younger sisters and brothers, and she'd be happy if she never saw another diaper or dust rag.

Mary Ann was one of the fortunate few black women who had a good education, and her family expected much of her. She planned to begin her career by teaching black children to read and write, to do their sums, and to find China and France and Russia on the map. She wanted them to know they were as good as anyone else. She was just the person to tell them.

2

Saying What She Thinks

Mary Ann began teaching in Wilmington when she was sixteen. During the next ten years, she taught in Delaware, New Jersey, Pennsylvania, and New York.

Mary Ann expected to be treated exactly like any other free American, and sometimes she was. One day in New York, where trolley cars usually did not stop to pick up black people, she waited at a trolley stop on Broadway. She stood proudly, head high, and waved at the driver as any white person would.

15

People on the street were surprised when the rough-looking driver stopped and let her on. Mary Ann wasn't surprised. She rode calmly to her destination.

Mary Ann often said, "We should do more, and talk less." She herself talked a lot, though. She wrote home from New Jersey in 1844, saying that she had a sore throat (probably from talking so much) and that she was having trouble with the black people there (probably they weren't doing what she said). Come home, her father wrote, where "you are welcome." By 1847, at age twenty-four, she was back home in West Chester, teaching.

In March 1849, in addition to talking and teaching, Mary Ann wrote to the famous black leader Frederick Douglass, telling him what should be done about the problems facing free blacks. She said black Americans should be self-reliant. They should own their own farms. We should be lifting ourselves up, she wrote, "not waiting for the whites of the country to do so." She stepped all over black preachers' toes by saying (in very strong words) that they were teaching "the free colored people of the North" to be submissive to whites. She said what "we most need" is the same knowledge the white man has. And, she said, "We should do more, and talk less." She signed it, "Yours for a better condition, M. A. Shadd."

Mr. Douglass published her letter in his newspaper *North Star,* and Mary Ann kept writing. That same year she published a twelve-page pamphlet called *Hints to the Colored People of the North.* She said she had to "expose every weakness" of her race in order to correct them. "How do [parades, fancy clothes, and public dinners] better our condition as a people?" she asked. Do not "set more value on the outside of the head than on what the inside needs," she said.

But hardly anyone bought her pamphlet. One person wrote to the *North Star,* saying that perhaps it contained "too much truth." Martin Delany, a black physician and abolitionist, said that Mary Ann was "a very intelligent young lady, and peculiarly eccentric."

Mary Ann did not behave the way women were supposed to. She wasn't quiet. She didn't stay home. She didn't depend on a man to make her decisions. No, Mary Ann said what she thought. And she thought every black person should have the same education, manners, and values that she had. This was the way to self-reliance and equality.

In 1850 the Fugitive Slave Law was passed as part of the Compromise of 1850 between the Northern and the Southern states. California was admitted to the Union as a free state—but Texas could have slavery.

Trading in slaves would be ended in Washington, D.C.—but runaway slaves (fugitives) would be captured and returned to their masters. It's "a business necessity," some Northern whites said. This new law made it easy for slave catchers to enter free states to hunt down fugitives and return them to their owners. Slave catchers were supposed to catch fugitive slaves only, but whether by mistake or on purpose, free blacks were sometimes seized as well.

By 1851 Mary Ann, age twenty-eight, was in New York City, teaching at Primary School No. 1 in the basement of a black church. Every day as she pinned on her hat and stepped out of her boardinghouse, she wondered if this might be the day she, or someone she knew, would be snatched off the street by a slave catcher. Would she end up as a slave in somebody's cotton field?

3

Canada

Ever since she was little, Mary Ann had heard about Canada, where there was no slavery and where blacks and whites were equals. She'd helped escaping slaves trying to get to Canada on the Underground Railroad. Mary Ann thought about moving there herself.

In September she went by train and steamship four hundred miles north to a convention in Toronto, a large, prosperous city in Canada on Lake Ontario. She wanted to learn more about life in Canada. There she met Henry Bibb, who had escaped from slavery eight years before. He lived safely in Windsor, Canada, just across Lake Erie from Detroit, Michigan. There, in the area known as Canada West, he published a newspaper, *Voice of the Fugitive*. Mr. Bibb told Mary Ann of the great need for teachers in Canada West. When she heard that, she knew what to do.

She packed her bags, bought a steamship ticket, straightened her shoulders and her hat, and sailed across Lake Erie to Windsor. She arrived in Canada full of hope and carrying her schoolbooks.

She found a "mud hole," a flat, forested, empty land where wagons, carts, and buggies sank so deep into the muddy roads that horses couldn't pull them. People needed bridges over the mud, but the part of town where black people lived had no bridges, no sidewalks, not even boards for people to walk on.

Mary Ann's shoulders sagged just a little when she saw how her people lived in Windsor. Where was the equality? She found a place to stay (in the black part of town), unpacked her books, and made notes on what to do first. There was more to fix than she'd thought.

Black farmers, blacksmiths, bricklayers, and businessmen had lived and worked peacefully in Windsor for years, she learned. But things had changed in 1850 when blacks fleeing the Fugitive Slave Law began arriving by the hundreds. Some of the new arrivals were free, educated blacks—but many more were fugitives who had never known any life but slavery. Windsor's white families did not want the new, poor, black children to go to school with their children. A law passed in 1850 stated that if black parents wanted their children to go to school, they had to ask for a separate school. Windsor's black parents *did* ask for a school, but the town couldn't find the money to build one.

So the black community had to make its own schools. Henry Bibb and his wife, Mary, believed it was best to have separate schools for blacks because the former slaves had never been in school before. They expected the new teacher, Miss Shadd, to agree with them.

She didn't.

Mary Ann had come to Canada to have the same rights as anyone else. She expected blacks to learn, and work, and go to church, and plow their fields next to whites. She could see that the white people in Canada were alarmed by the great number of fugitive slaves. She knew what to do about it.

Mary Ann waded through the mud to the Bibbs' house for a talk. She told them she "*would not* teach" in a school for blacks only. Children should not be separated by a "complexional difference," she said. How can we live together as equals, she asked, when we are separated by skin color? How will whites and blacks ever get to know each other?

Mary Ann set out to find a place for her school. She found a bare room in an old military barracks, with a few wobbly benches and an iron stove. The barracks had been built for soldiers during the War of 1812. It was a wreck, but it was the best place she could find, so she cleaned it out and made it do.

She opened her school for everyone, but only black students came—thirteen children in the daytime and eleven adults at night—students from age four to age thirty-three. They were each to pay three shillings a month, about fifty cents, and to provide firewood. Unfortunately, few paid.

She lowered the tuition to thirty-seven cents a month. Still few paid. Mary Ann soon had no income at all. Her own parents sent her money for food. But, she said, the important thing is "the fugitives are anxious to learn." She knew many white people thought former slaves could never learn enough to be self-reliant, and she was going to prove them wrong.

Then winter blew in, leaving Miss Shadd and her students in "a very cold, open [room], unfurnished & objectionable in every way." She had no money *and* a frozen classroom. She had to close her school and ask for help.

She wrote to the American Missionary Association (AMA) in New York City, which already had some teachers in Canada West. Mary Ann told AMA secretary George Whipple, a white man, about her work and asked for help—$250 for the year.

Mr. Whipple asked for more information. A white AMA missionary in Windsor, Rev. Alexander McArthur, wrote that Mary Ann Shadd was a young light-colored lady with a fine education, lots of energy, and should be helped. Mr. Whipple still hesitated. He asked about her church life. Mary Ann said she had left the African Methodist Episcopal Church because it was a "complexion church"—for blacks only. And, so Mr. Whipple wouldn't ask, she ended her letter, "I am unmarried."

By January 1852, she had not heard from the AMA, but the weather improved. She reopened her classroom in the dismal barracks and began teaching reading, math, and geography again.

Finally, she received good news. The AMA agreed to pay her a salary—$125 for one year. The students' parents were to pay the rest. Mary Ann wasn't sure how much the parents would pay (she received only $2 in January), but she could buy books, paper, pencils, and firewood with the $125. "Please accept my thanks," she wrote.

Mary Ann taught all day and all evening, and still she found the time to write a forty-four-page book.

She had heard what Southern slave owners told their slaves to keep them from escaping. In Canada, they said, your eyes will be poked out, you will be skinned alive, and your children will be eaten. So her book, *Notes of Canada West,* told blacks in the United States the truth about Canada.

Mary Ann had the book printed by a white printer in Detroit. He added some words of his own, made mistakes, and would not listen to her complaints. She wished she had never taken her book to him. Even worse, Henry Bibb scolded her in his newspaper for choosing a white American printer. She should have spent her money in the black community, he said. Mr. Bibb did say, though, that the free black people of the United States should read Mary Ann's book so they would know "what to do."

The book came out in 1852 and cost twelve cents. It was packed with information about schools, laws, churches, money, jobs, and the weather. Don't worry about the winters, Mary Ann said. Many towns in Canada are farther south than parts of "Maine, New Hampshire, Vermont, New York, Michigan, and Oregon." She said if black settlers worked hard, "with an axe and a little energy," they would soon be independent. It wasn't quite as easy as she said, but Mary Ann thought a good way to self-reliance was to own farmland. It's true, she said, that even in Canada a black person might be treated badly. Still, she said, Canada is far better than "a miserable scampering from state to state," keeping one step ahead of the slave catcher.

People who read her book said that Mary Ann knew the facts about black life in Canada. But the Bibbs, who thought they should be the ones to talk about Canada, were not pleased.

Meanwhile, in June 1852, the new president of the United States, Franklin Pierce, promised slave owners he would use the full power of the government to carry out the Fugitive Slave Law. "I believe that [slavery] is recognized by the Constitution," he said. The Fugitive Slave Law "should be respected and obeyed . . . cheerfully."

At that, Mary Ann's father gave up on living peacefully as a free black man in the United States. He traveled to Windsor, visited his daughter, and bought farmland. Then he went back to Pennsylvania to collect his family and several other families who were moving to Canada West.

4

A Terrible Year

Mary Ann found herself in trouble. Mr. and Mrs. Bibb, it seemed, wanted to cut Mary Ann Shadd down to a proper, silent, submissive-to-her-betters size.

Even though many of her school's families were terribly poor, Mary Ann thought they should pay for their education so they'd appreciate it more and feel self-reliant. She had not yet told them that the AMA was going to pay $125 as part of her salary. But Mr. Bibb told them, in his newspaper.

Mary Ann was horrified. People would think she was dishonest. She was sure Henry Bibb had done this on purpose. She wrote the AMA that she had planned to tell people about the money "when the school should be firmly established—a few weeks." She was so embarrassed and outraged that her letter went on for four pages. When she ran out of paper, she wrote between the lines she'd already written and along the sides.

And there was more to worry about. Mr. Bibb and some white men from the AMA had started the Refugee Home Society to buy land in Canada. Fugitive slaves would then buy land from the society. But Mary Ann saw new buildings going up on land the Bibbs owned—and they owned more and more land. She feared the Bibbs were taking land meant for the fugitives.

The society also sent out men, black and white, to ask for money and old clothes for the fugitives. Mary Ann called them "beggars." Her face burned with shame at the idea of begging. She knew white people would think black people couldn't take care of themselves if they had to be given money and old clothes. This isn't right, she said. We are *equals,* not inferior, helpless, dependent people.

She stormed back to Mr. Bibb. Fugitives need to buy land and begin farming, she said. They do not need white people's old clothes. We must behave like equals, she said.

Henry Bibb told her the Refugee Home Society was his idea. He said begging was necessary because the fugitives arrived with nothing. He said the society had to sell and control the land because the fugitives didn't know how.

People respected Mr. Bibb and his paper. He was a

former slave himself. Miss Shadd, however, was a light-skinned, educated, free black woman. Some people said she couldn't possibly understand the needs of fugitive slaves.

The AMA and other white abolitionist groups, along with the black community in Canada, believed what Mr. Bibb wrote about Mary Ann. The white men who ran the AMA and the Refugee Home Society thought begging was the best way to raise money. They were already unhappy with the out-spoken, fiery Miss Shadd.

Once again Mary Ann wrote to the AMA secretary, Mr. Whipple, to explain herself. When she ran out of room she wrote sideways, "I have not a paper of my own and must leave the result with God." Then she thought about what she'd just written. Why couldn't she have a paper of her own? Mary Ann began a new list—things to do, people to talk to, facts to find on how to publish and pay for a newspaper. First, though, she had to explain the $125.

The community met at Mary Ann's school on July 20, 1852, a hot and sticky day. The school's families listened to her explanation, and, to Mary Ann's relief, they agreed with everything she had done.

The very next day a white man visited her school. He wrote to the AMA that Miss Shadd "is a very capable young woman." He agreed that the fugitives should not be treated as if they were helpless.

That same hot summer, the Reverend Samuel Ringgold Ward arrived in Windsor with his wife and five children. Rev. Ward was born a slave and had escaped to freedom with his parents when he was a child. He was well educated, a minister, an abolitionist, and a gifted speaker. He, too, was fleeing the Fugitive Slave Law. Rev. Ward had already written some words against the Refugee Home Society: "The world knows the difference between a class of beggars and a class of workers." After listening to Mary Ann's worries, he called a meeting to discuss the society's problems. Many of the men who came said that begging insulted them. We can take care of ourselves, they said. Abolitionists in the United States should stop sending clothes and money.

Then Mary Ann's words against begging were printed in the *Liberator,* one of the most famous abolitionist papers in the United States. But a white Presbyterian minister, Rev. C. C. Foote, who raised thousands of dollars for the society by telling white people how the helpless fugitives were suffering, said Mary Ann didn't know the truth of slavery. He and another minister, Rev. John Scoble, told the AMA to stop supporting her school.

Rev. McArthur, the white missionary, wrote to Mr. Whipple. Mr. Bibb "is fast realizing a fortune," he wrote. Miss Shadd, however, "has led a blameless life . . . you could not find a better teacher."

Mary Ann cleared a space on her table and began her own letter to the confused Mr. Whipple. "Henry Bibb," she wrote, "has hundreds of dollars belonging to fugitives, probably thousands would be nearer the truth." And now, she thought, the truth was out.

Autumn was lovely in Windsor. The dirt roads were dry and smooth, the harvest was good, and Mary Ann's school started again. She added history and botany to her list of subjects. She was pleased to say that finally she had "children of all complexions."

Mary Ann's parents had bought a farm in Buxton, only a pleasant day or two's buggy ride away from Windsor. The community began building a new schoolhouse with two rooms, one for classes and one for the teacher's home. And in December 1852, the AMA reported that Miss Shadd, age twenty-nine, was an "experienced colored teacher" whose work was "full and satisfactory."

Mary Ann smiled to herself as she thought how well things were going. She hurried through the snow to her classroom each day, eager to light the fire in the stove and get the day's lessons ready.

One month later the AMA fired her, supposedly for her "religious views." Mary Ann read Mr. Whipple's letter over and over. She felt as if someone had hit her. She knew she'd been fired because she'd found things going wrong and would not be quiet about it, because she would not obey the men in charge, because she said what she thought and would not back down.

Mary Ann no longer trusted white ministers. They have, she said, "smooth words, and hearts full of negro-hate." But she was polite. She thanked the AMA for its past help and mailed the letter. It was time for her to do something she'd been thinking about all that year.

4

A Newspaper of Her Own

In March 1853, Mary Ann became the first black woman to publish a weekly newspaper. She called it the *Provincial Freeman* and said the first issue on March 24 was a sample of what was to come. Send letters, said the paper, to "Mary A. Shadd, Windsor, Canada West." Two important men, Rev. Samuel Ringgold Ward and Rev. Alexander McArthur, were named as editors.

This new paper, Rev. Ward wrote in the first issue, "will be devoted to the elevation of the Colored People." It would be for the black community and its white neighbors. It would publish local news, world news, and readers' letters. It would print both sides of problems so "our readers may judge." It would be a place where Mary Ann could say what she thought.

She wanted the *Freeman* to show fugitives how to be self-reliant, free women and men. First, though, the *Freeman* itself had to be self-reliant. So Mary Ann said the paper would be published every week as soon as there were enough subscribers who promised to pay $1.50 a year.

Rev. Ward sailed to England to talk to white audiences there about slavery. And Mary Ann set out to raise money for her new paper. She went to Philadelphia and gave talks about Canada and her newspaper. Black groups and white groups listened with great interest to a woman speaking in public. They were surprised at how young she was—still only twenty-nine—and how cleverly she gave the facts. She even used a large map of North America to make her points clear. Her eyes sparkled as she told people about the *Provincial Freeman* and took down names of subscribers.

Meanwhile, she decided to move east, from Windsor to Toronto. More than one thousand black people lived there, and Mary Ann hoped they would all buy her newspaper.

For one whole year, Mary Ann talked about the *Freeman*. By March 1854, she had enough subscribers to begin publication.

Rev. Ward was still in England and Rev. McArthur was on his way to Scotland, but it was Mary Ann Shadd's paper. She put "Self-Reliance is the True Road to Independence" at the top of the front page and wrote her articles carefully. She chose her printer carefully, too—he was an Englishman who had worked with Frederick Douglass. This paper, Mary Ann said, would correct two great lies—that black people were unfit for freedom and that blacks could not live as equals with whites. Her first weekly newspaper was published in Toronto on Saturday, March 25, 1854, and mailed to its subscribers.

Mary Ann had no idea when Rev. Ward would return, but she kept his name as editor. She was afraid she would lose readers if people knew a woman was in charge. Readers were told to send letters to M. A. Shadd, "during the absence of the Editor." Mary Ann wasn't all alone, though. Several men helped by contributing articles and money. One of these men was Thomas F. Cary, a black businessman and friend of Rev. Ward. Mr. Cary was, said Rev. Ward, "one of the sincerest, most generous, practical friends I ever had." Mr. Cary owned barbershops in Toronto and went to many of the same meetings as Mary Ann. They thought alike, and they began working together to start a group for black self-reliance.

Mary Ann's office was in a brick building on King Street in the middle of busy downtown Toronto. Most days she sat at her desk writing articles and choosing items from other papers that she hoped would uplift the former slaves. She printed tips for keeping a clean house and a neat farm, recipes on "how to boil and dress maccaroni," stories by Charles Dickens, poems, and complaints. She went to meetings and lectures and reported on them for her readers. (But it would be better, she said, if people went themselves.) She tried to get black women involved in working together and speaking out as *she* did.

She scolded those whose writing didn't come up to her standards. "A waste of time," she said about one letter. Have "a beginning and an end," she said to another writer, and "please write plainly." (One man finally wrote to complain of the editor's "fire flashes.") But people kept writing. "Our table is literally groaning" under the weight of letters, she wrote happily.

There were many letters, agreeing and disagreeing, but not much money. Mary Ann was angry and offended when whites in Toronto raised money for Frederick Douglass's paper in the United States, not for Mary Ann's paper in Canada. Douglass said blacks should not move to Canada. Was that what the Toronto folks wanted? she asked angrily.

In July 1854, Mary Ann visited a black community not far from Windsor. Rev. John Scoble, the white minister who had gotten her fired as a teacher, was in charge of helping fugitives there, and she wanted to see what was going on. She found ragged men and women living in terrible conditions, not at all self-reliant. She immediately wrote articles on what she saw and sent them back to the *Freeman.*

She was talking about self-reliance at a meeting in a log schoolhouse when Rev. Scoble roared in. He had seen her articles. He told the black community "that they could not afford to lose any of their friends," and they *would* lose them if the *Freeman* didn't stop its attacks. He stamped his foot, pointed his finger at Mary Ann, and warned her to be careful, as the people against her were "very powerful."

But Rev. Scoble had run into a rock. "You might as well attempt to move a stone wall with your little finger," one man said, as to try and stop Mary Ann Shadd.

"The fact that somebody is displeased," Mary Ann wrote calmly in her next article, "is no evidence that we are wrong." In fact, she had no doubt she was right. She kept telling the fugitives how to be self-reliant and think for themselves. Begging only helped "the men who beg for the fugitives—who live by the trade," she wrote. And, as she often wrote when she ran out of space, "we shall examine this subject more fully next week."

In August 1854, a man in Michigan wrote, "May the Lord bless you, brother Shadd!" Mary Ann shook her head. The time had come to tell her readers that M. A. Shadd was actually Mary Ann Shadd. And not only was one woman publishing the *Freeman*—*two* women were. Mary Ann's sister Amelia, age twenty-three, had come to help, for neither Rev. Ward nor Rev. McArthur had returned. In October the men's names were removed from the paper.

Meanwhile, the bills were piling up. Mary Ann went by train to speak in Michigan, Ohio, and Pennsylvania, selling copies of *Notes of Canada West* to pay her way. It was a hard trip, and she was often insulted by whites. She would grit her teeth, hold her head high, and walk on. Mary Ann had to raise money to pay the printer, and she meant to do it.

She also had to collect money from her subscribers. This was difficult when the roads were sloppy with mud and the trees bent in the wind. She carried her papers and her umbrella, held her long skirts out of the mud, and kept her chin up and her hat firmly on her head. One man who saw her out in bad weather said everyone respected her hard work.

Well, not everyone. Mary Ann was puzzled that many black women weren't helpful to her. The more she thought about it, the angrier she felt. So she wrote about the "muslin multitude," the "delicate creatures" who show only "nothingness." Alas, these sharp words didn't make women any more helpful.

"That many persons do not like the *Freeman,* we know full well," Mary Ann wrote in June 1855. She knew why—its editor was a woman. There was another reason, too—she often offended readers with her impatience.

Mary Ann's brother Isaac came to help. He would be the new publisher, and Rev. William Newman of Toronto would be the new editor. Mary Ann took her own and Amelia's names off the paper. "The ladies will be pleased," Mary Ann said, and they might even help raise money.

She wrote, "To colored women, we have a word—we have broken the Editorial ice . . . so go to Editing, as many of you as are willing, and able." Maybe *this* would inspire the "muslin multitude" to help her. Maybe some would even take her advice and go into business themselves.

Toronto was an expensive city—too expensive. Mary Ann and Isaac packed up their old printing press and moved west to Chatham, close to their parents'

farm in Buxton. Mary Ann could save money by living with her family. Best of all, many successful black
farmers and businesspeople lived nearby, and they
would want her paper. Yes, she decided, Chatham was
the best home for the *Freeman*.

Then Mary Ann went back on the road, writing articles and trying to raise money and subscribers for the
Freeman. Her articles were a great success. Her
fundraising was not. Times were hard, and people
had little money left over for a paper. Back in
Chatham, week after week, Isaac Shadd asked subscribers to pay for the paper. Pay even in "bread and
cheese, and wood," he said, though he would "rather
have the cash!"

Editor Newman, meanwhile, tried to smooth feel-
ings that were hurt by Mary Ann's sharp and critical
pen. He thought the paper needed the support and
money of white folks, including missionaries. But
Mary Ann wanted nothing to do with white missionaries, and her pen would not be quiet. She wrote
angrily about the "despotic, dictatorial, snobbish air
of superiority of white people over the fugitives."
What we really need from the white man, she wrote,
is "the knowledge that makes him so potent."

Mary Ann wanted to remind her readers what was
going on in the United States. She printed ads from

Southern papers: For Sale: "A negro woman 36 years old, $780; a negro boy 7 or 8 years old, $700; and a negro boy child, only 4 years old, $330."

For Sale: "City bonds, railroad stock, Negro Man," and a half-white slave woman sold by her own father (her master) for $1,100.

She printed a letter from a former slave. "I now take *my pen* to write to you," the woman began, "I say my pen, because I *own* something. . . . The pen is mine and not 'Old Mistress's.'"

Mary Ann ran ads for hats, bonnets, furs; for boots and shoes; for a hotel with a stable for horses. She listed daily wages for different kinds of work: brick-layer, $1.50–$2; painter, $1–$1.50. To help her readers, she printed the daily schedule of the Great Western Railway from Windsor to Niagara Falls. What more could she do?

6

Change and More Change

In October 1855, Mary Ann went to Philadelphia for the Colored National Convention. She arrived worn out from traveling and tired of standing up to rude conductors. She was the only delegate from Canada.

The first day, Mary Ann asked for ten minutes to talk about life in Canada. She glanced at her notes, cleared her throat, and began. At the end of ten minutes, the men were so interested they let her continue. She spoke for an hour to a very attentive audience. Then she folded her notes and left the platform. "She is a superior woman, and it is useless to deny it," said a man from Brooklyn.

Isaiah Wears, a black abolitionist and a "most logical, ready, reliable, and eloquent debater," did not agree with Mary Ann about blacks emigrating to Canada. He challenged her to a debate. Mary Ann smiled and got ready to have fun.

When it was her turn, she laid out her facts clearly. Then she said Mr. Wears couldn't pin down the issue. This reminded her of trying to catch a flea, she said, for "when he went to put his finger on it, it was not there."

The men listening roared with laughter, which didn't help Mr. Wears. When the debate was over, Mary Ann had won.

Three nights later, people in Philadelphia honored Mary Ann at a special fundraising program with speeches and music and ice cream. She had a wonderful time, and she was amazed and happy to be given $75 for her newspaper.

Soon she was even happier. She had decided that Thomas Cary, a man she'd worked with over the years, was a man worth marrying.

Thomas and Mary Ann were married in January 1856 at her sister Amelia's home. Mary Ann immediately became a stepmother to John, age seven; Thomas Jr., eleven; and Ann, fourteen. Thomas knew Mary Ann's passion for justice. He knew she would keep writing, speaking, and traveling. He knew he would not have an ordinary wife (or life), so he kept his house and barbershop business in Toronto, and he traveled many hard miles back and forth to Chatham.

Soon after her wedding, Mary Ann left to get more subscribers for the paper. This time she headed for Chicago, Illinois, where it was thirty degrees below zero. She wrapped up in hat and coat, scarves and shawls, traveled by sleigh and by train, and spoke in churches and halls all over Illinois, Wisconsin, and Michigan. She even preached sermons. Excellent sermons, one listener said. A superior mind, said another.

Mary Ann returned to Chatham in May 1856 with a bold idea. "Cease to uphold the United States government," she wrote in the *Freeman,* "while it upholds human slavery." She wanted people to pay attention.

Frederick Douglass paid attention. On July 4, he wrote that Mary Ann Shadd is "unconquerable." And, he went on, "we do not know her equal among the colored ladies of the United States." (He also said her writing at times was a bit "harsh.")

Mary Ann glowed with happiness and pride. But she wished that Mr. Douglass had spoken these words (most of them, anyway) a little earlier.

Meanwhile, Chatham continued to grow. The black abolitionist Dr. Martin Delany arrived with his family. Miss Amelia Freeman from Pittsburgh came to Chatham to "give instruction in painting, drawing, music, writing, etc."

Mary Ann began helping Miss Freeman at her school. The "little colored school house" was a disgrace, Mary Ann wrote in her newspaper. Eighty students were crowded into a small wooden building without a stove, maps, or globes. This was an insult to colored people, Mary Ann said.

But every day she walked to that miserable schoolhouse with her head high. Every day she taught, every evening she wrote, and every night she worried about bills.

Thomas sold oil lamps and ice, in addition to his barbering. Still there was barely enough money to buy paper and ink for the newspaper or clothes for the family.

In January 1857, Mary Ann sat at her desk, thinking about what to write for the new year. She was disgusted with white missionaries who kept asking for help for the fugitives. There are German and Irish and others in need too, she wrote, and no one begs for old clothes for *them.* Only the black folks are considered helpless, she said.

She wrote about the vast sums of money that had been begged for the fugitives, for schools, for churches—enough money to build "an empire," she said. But people could see how dismal the schools and churches were.

In February, with bills spilling off her desk, she stared at the blank paper in front of her. Her throat was tight with bitterness. She began to write, faster and faster, her pen almost tearing the paper. Why do you not pay what you owe us? she asked her subscribers. Why do you pay the white man first? Why do even *you* consider the white man more important?

Spring rainstorms raged outside her window, and thunder shook the brick walls. Whole blocks of old wooden buildings, which were lit by candles, caught fire and burned to the ground. Mary Ann reported it all in her paper. She probably felt like burning her bills in the fire, too.

Mary Ann argued with the pastors of Chatham's white churches. Black Christians were not invited to "enter their doors," she said. "What will those white Christian souls do in Heaven?" She argued with men over women's rights. "Some Men," she said, "foolishly deny to a Woman the right to speak in public, to practice medicine, or to vote." She argued with Chatham's leaders over whom to vote for in town elections. Then she stopped arguing.

Her first baby, Sarah, was born in August 1857. Mary Ann and Thomas were proud, happy, and much too busy to worry about arguing with anybody.

In early 1858, Thomas wrote to Mary Ann from

Toronto, where he'd gone to check on his barber-shops. "Give my love to the Children," he said, "and Kiss the baby." He enclosed seven dollars, all the money he had.

All their hard work wasn't enough. Mary Ann couldn't keep her newspaper alive and pay the family's bills, too. A few issues of the *Freeman* came out in 1858, along with a notice that "the debts must be paid!"

John Brown, a white American abolitionist, came to Chatham in 1858. He met with Mary Ann's brother and husband and a few other men to discuss his idea to "strike down slavery." Mary Ann undoubtedly met him, too, but she didn't write about it.

Meanwhile, although Martin Delany had written proudly that Mary Ann's paper had "a much larger circulation among the colored people than *Frederick Douglass' Paper,*" the *Provincial Freeman* was fading away. The last issue was printed in June 1859.

7

A New Life

Mary Ann's husband fell ill, and her newspaper still owed money. Somehow she had to feed their children. She sat at her desk and wrote articles. She went out to speak. She helped at the school. It wasn't enough. She grimly wrote to a friend that they "live along partly on the bounty of relatives."

In November 1860, Thomas died. A few weeks later Mary Ann's second baby, a boy she named Linton, was born.

In March 1861, Abraham Lincoln became president of the United States. He would not give in to Southerners over the problem of slavery. One month later, the North (the Union) and the South (the Confederacy) went to war.

In Canada, life was not what Mary Ann had dreamed it would be. Black farmers found their fences pulled down, their horses and hogs stolen, their crops destroyed. Black workers could not get jobs. But French, Irish, and German immigrants could.

Mary Ann's three teenage stepchildren went to Haiti with their uncle, who thought life would be better there. Three weeks later he died from a fever, and the three children disappeared.

Mary Ann missed Thomas. She thought of her two children without a father. She thought of just doing nothing for a while. But then she thought of the "muslin multitude" doing nothing, and she shuddered.

In December 1863, Mary Ann received a letter from Martin Delany. He was in Chicago, Illinois, signing up black men to fight for the Union army in the Civil War, and he asked Mary Ann to help. She would be paid. It would be a dangerous job, and it was just what she needed. She packed a bag and left her children with her parents.

Mary Ann was one of very few black women to be a Union army recruiter. She spoke all over the northern United States, encouraging black men to fight for the Union. She heard threats and insults from vengeful whites every day. Sparks flew from Mary Ann's eyes, but she stayed calm and did her job well. Thousands of blacks joined the Union army.

In the spring of 1865, the Civil War ended. The South was defeated, every slave was freed, and Mary

Ann returned to Canada. She thought about what to do next. Her parents and most of her family were going to stay in Canada. Two of her brothers, Isaac and Abraham, had gone back to the United States. Mary Ann decided to take her children, her Canadian passport, and go home to the United States, too.

In 1869 Mary Ann Shadd Cary arrived in Washington, D.C., with Sarah, age twelve, and Linton, age eight. Washington was bursting with energy and excitement. The huge red brick Smithsonian Castle was completed. The Mall had beautiful gardens and buildings. Row houses lined noisy streets clogged with horses, wagons, and buggies. A forest of ships' masts rose from the Potomac River. Here, Mary Ann hoped, she could find new ways to fight for justice. She taught all day. She worked all evening as the principal of a night school for former slaves.

In the fall of 1869, at the age of forty-six, she became the first black woman to enter law school— Howard University Law School. She wrote to her sister Amelia that the men weren't too happy about it. "There is some squirming among some students," she wrote, "but I care not. I have an end to accomplish."

Something went wrong, though. The first class of law students graduated in February 1871. Mary Ann Cary should have been in it, but she was not. A second group graduated in July 1871. Mary Ann Cary was not in it. She said later that Howard University had decided not to award a law degree to a woman. Not yet, anyway.

Meanwhile, she took on another fight. In 1871 she and sixty-two other women, black and white, tried to vote. They were turned away. So Mary Ann wrote "A First Vote Almost." In her article, she poked fun at a man who, she said, was shocked at the sight of women pushing right through a crowd of men. "Ought to be hoss whipped," he said, as he "sighs for a return of the good old times."

Mary Ann started a black women's group. She worked for women's rights and argued for the vote. She fought for jobs for black workers. She kept writing articles. She wanted to open a bank to make loans to black businesses. She wanted people to listen.

She was angry that, as a black person, she still did not have the same rights as whites. "Wherever we go we carry our color with us," she said. She was bitter that, as a woman, she did not have the same rights as a man. She was sad that her work was not recognized like that of Frederick Douglass or Susan B. Anthony, a white woman who fought for women's rights. She knew she had offended everybody. "Can't help it," she said.

And still she was unconquerable. In May 1883, Mary Ann received her law degree. She was sixty years old. "M. A. Shadd Cary, Esq., a colored lady lawyer," proudly practiced law the rest of her life, and with every case she took, she fought for justice.

Mary Ann died at her daughter Sarah's home in Washington in June 1893. One small article cut from a newspaper was found with her things, worn and folded. Perhaps she read it whenever she felt discouraged and forgotten. It began, "Mrs. Mary Shadd Cary, one of the most talented colored women of the country . . ."

The Washington *Bee* said, "While she may have been eccentric at times . . . she was a woman of excellent traits of character." And Frederick Douglass wrote the truest truth—Mary Ann Shadd Cary was "a pioneer among colored women."

Afterword

Mary Ann Shadd Cary spent her life fighting for justice for her people, for the same rights as any other person had, for equality. In the 1920s, American women got the vote. In the 1960s, black Americans were finally granted some of the rights Mary Ann had fought for in the 1860s.

She challenged what people thought and how they acted. She demanded that whites look past "complexional differences." She believed it was her right and duty to speak up when she saw wrongdoing, and she fought all her life to be listened to. She worked with men to solve problems that other women wouldn't tackle. She scolded and challenged people—important people—in public and in print. She was just plain stubborn.

Mary Ann's whole life was lived on the edge—on the edge of white society, on the edge of true freedom, on the edge of men's rights, on the edge of poverty, on the edge between bitterness and joy. In the years to come, other brave black women, such as Ida B. Wells-Barnett, Mary Church Terrell, and Mary McLeod Bethune, would step forward to carry on her fight for justice in word and in action.

But Mary Ann Shadd Cary went first.

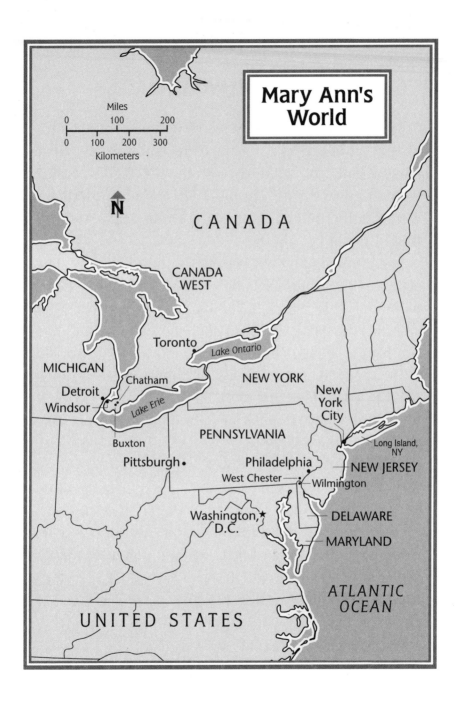

Mary Ann's World

Miles
0   100   200

0   100   200   300
Kilometers

N

CANADA

CANADA
WEST

Toronto

Lake Ontario

MICHIGAN

Chatham

NEW YORK

Detroit

New
York
City

Windsor

Lake Erie

Buxton

PENNSYLVANIA

Long Island,
NY

Pittsburgh

Philadelphia

NEW JERSEY

West Chester

Wilmington

Washington,
D.C.

DELAWARE

MARYLAND

ATLANTIC
OCEAN

UNITED STATES

Selected Bibliography
Selected Books and Articles

Bearden, Jim, and Linda Jean Butler. *Shadd: The Life and Times of Mary Shadd Cary.* Toronto: NC Press, 1977.

Brown, Hallie Q. *Homespun Heroines.* New York: Oxford University Press, 1988.

Hancock, Harold B. "Mary Ann Shadd: Negro Editor, Educator, and Lawyer." *Delaware History Magazine*, 1973, 187–194.

Hutton, Frankie. *The Early Black Press in America, 1827 to 1860.* London: Greenwood Press, 1993.

Murray, Alexander L. "The Provincial Freeman." *Journal of Negro History,* April 1959, 123–135.

Peterson, Carla L. *"Doers of the Word": African American Women Speakers & Writers in the North (1830–1880).* New York: Oxford University Press, 1995.

Rhodes, Jane. *Mary Ann Shadd Cary: The Black Press and Protest in the Nineteenth Century.* Bloomington, IN: Indiana University Press, 1998.

Robinson, Gwen. *Seek the Truth: A Story of Chatham's Black Community.* Chatham, 1989.

Sadlier, Rosemary. *Mary Ann Shadd.* Toronto: Umbrella Press, 1995.

Shadd, Ruth Ann. *Cousins by the Dozens.* Booklet, 2000.

Streitmatter, Rodger. *Raising Her Voice: African-American Women Journalists Who Changed History.* Lexington, KY: University Press of Kentucky, 1994.

Winks, Robin W. *The Blacks in Canada: A History.* New Haven, CT: Yale University Press, 1971.

Documents and Newspapers

Cary, Mary Ann Shadd. Letter to Amelia, Sept. 5, 1869, Washington, D.C.

Douglass, Frederick. Letter to Mary Ann Shadd Cary, July 4, 1891, Rochester, NY.

Provincial Freeman, 1854–1858 (microfilms of originals, Smith College Library, subscription of Martin Delaney).

Shadd, Mary Ann. Letter to Frederick Douglass/*The North Star*, Jan. 25, 1849. Wilmington, Delaware.

Williamson, Amelia Shadd. "Record of the Shadd Family in America," 1905.

Interviews

Gwen Robinson, Artis Lane, Dorothy Shadd Shreve (family); Dr. Berky Nelson, UCLA; Dr. Jane Rhodes, UCSD.

Websites

The Black Community in the History of Quebec and Canada
<http://www.qesnrecit.qc.ca/mpages/unit3/u3p68.htm>

Notices in the Provincial Freeman
<http://www.iath.virginia.edu/utc/africam/pfhp.html>

Provincial Freeman—Archives of Ontario
<http://www.archives.gov.on.ca/english/exhibits/humnrits/pic9.htm>

Index

Abolitionists, 7, 11, 17, 30, 31, 46, 52
American Missionary Association (AMA), 23–24, 28, 30, 33, 34

Bibb, Henry, 19–20, 21, 26, 27, 28–29
Brown, John, 52
Buxton, Canada West, 33, 43

Canada, 7, 9, 19, 21, 26–27, 29, 54
Cary, Linton (son), 53, 55
Cary, Mary Ann Shadd:
birth, 5; childhood, 7–13; determination, 41; education, 11–13, 55, 57; publishing, 35–39; talking, 16, 17, 36, 46–48, 49; teaching, 13–14, 18, 23–24, 32–33, 50, 55; writing, 16, 24–26, 28, 30, 39, 44, 50–51, 57
Cary, Sarah (daughter), 51–52, 55, 58
Cary, Thomas (husband), 38, 48, 50, 51–53
Chatham, Canada West, 43–44, 48, 52
Civil War, 53–54
Colored National Convention, 46–48

Delany, Martin, 17, 49, 52, 54
Douglass, Frederick, 16, 38, 39, 49, 52, 57, 58

Equality, 9, 19, 21, 29, 38, 39, 59

Free blacks, 5, 6–7, 10–11, 16, 20, 30, 54
Freeman, Amelia, 49–50
Fugitives, 7–9, 18, 20–21, 29, 36, 41, 50
Fugitive Slave Law, 17, 20, 27, 31

Hints to the Colored People of the North, 17
Howard University Law School, 55, 57

Liberator, 31

McArthur, Rev. Alexander, 24, 33, 35, 38, 42

New York City, 14–16, 18
Newman, Rev. William, 43, 44
North Star, 17, 39
Notes of Canada West, 26, 42

Philadelphia, Pennsylvania, 10–13, 36, 46, 48
Provincial Freeman, 35–39, 41–45, 49, 52

Refugee Home Society, 29–31
Runaway slaves. *See* Fugitives

Scoble, Rev. John, 31, 41
Self-reliance, 5, 16–17, 26–27, 38, 41

Shadd, Abraham (father), 6–7, 9–10, 11, 16, 27

Shadd, Amelia (sister), 42, 48, 55

Shadd, Harriet (mother), 7, 10

Shadd, Isaac (brother), 43, 52, 54

Shadd, Mary Ann. *See* Cary, Mary Ann Shadd

Slavery, 10, 17–18, 27, 44–45, 49, 53, 54

Toronto, Canada West, 19, 36, 38–39, 43, 48

Underground Railroad, 7–9

Voting rights, 51, 56–57, 59

Ward, Rev. Samuel Ringgold, 31, 35, 36, 38, 42

Washington, D.C., 55

Wears, Isaiah, 46–48

West Chester, Pennsylvania, 10–11, 16

Whipple, George, 24, 30, 33, 34

Wilmington, Delaware, 6–7, 14

Windsor, Canada West, 19–21, 27

Recent Honors

Mary Ann Shadd Cary residence (from 1881–1886), 1421 W Street N.W., Washington, D.C., declared a National Monument in 1976.

Mary Ann Shadd Cary inducted into the Hall of Fame for Delaware Women in Dover, Delaware, March 19, 1997.

Mary Ann Shadd Cary inducted into the National Women's Hall of Fame in Seneca Falls, New York, July 11, 1998.